Psychology Revivals

The Troubled Conscience and the Insane Mind

Originally published in 1928 in the *Psyche Miniatures Medical Series*, this title was an attempt to bring to the attention of British psychologists and psychiatrists some aspects of the work and thought of French psychologist Charles Blondel. Well known abroad but little known in England at the time, he was professor of Psychology at the University of Strasbourg and founder of a school of 'morbid psychology'.

This book contains two papers, the first concerning the theory of the disordered mind and the second deals with the relation between disordered thought and speech. Today it can be read and enjoyed in its historical context.

The Troubled Conscience and the Insane Mind

Charles Blondel

Routledge
Taylor & Francis Group
LONDON AND NEW YORK

First published in 1928
by Kegan Paul, Trench, Trubner & Co. Ltd

This edition first published in 2014 by Routledge
27 Church Road, Hove, BN3 2FA

and by Routledge
711 Third Avenue, New York, NY 10017

Routledge is an imprint of the Taylor & Francis Group, an informa business

Publisher's Note
The publisher has gone to great lengths to ensure the quality of this reprint but points out that some imperfections in the original copies may be apparent.

Disclaimer
The publisher has made every effort to trace copyright holders and welcomes correspondence from those they have been unable to contact.

ISBN: 978-0-415-74174-3 (hbk)
ISBN: 978-1-315-81443-8 (ebk)

PSYCHE MINIATURES
Medical Series, No. 10

THE TROUBLED CONSCIENCE AND THE INSANE MIND

THE TROUBLED CONSCIENCE

AND THE INSANE MIND

BY

CHARLES BLONDEL

Professor of Psychology in the University of Strasbourg
Correspondant de l'Institut

WITH AN INTRODUCTION BY

F. G. CROOKSHANK

M.D., F.R.C.P.

Author of "Migraine and Other Common Neuroses," etc.

LONDON

KEGAN PAUL, TRENCH, TRUBNER & Co., Ltd.

BROADWAY HOUSE, CARTER LANE, E.C.

1928

Printed in Great Britain by
R. I. SEVERS, CAMBRIDGE

CONTENTS

INTRODUCTION

In this volume of the PSYCHE MINIATURES an attempt is made to bring before British psychologists and psychiatrists some aspects of the work and thought—well-known abroad: little known in England—of Charles Blondel, professor of Psychology in the University of Strasbourg, and himself the founder of an active school of "morbid psychology".

Briefly: the work of Blondel has been directed towards the better understanding of *la conscience morbide*, or the insane mind; and in order that it may be appreciated, selection has here been made of two papers from the distinguished author's pen. Of these, the first was written for delivery as a special lecture, at Geneva in 1922, under the title of *La Conscience Morbide*, and in explanation, or exposition, of an earlier and much longer essay, published under the same name, on the eve of the outbreak of the Great War. It is this latter essay which contains the full setting-out of that theory of the disordered mind with which Blondel's name is definitely connected.

The second paper here translated and presented should be considered as exegetical in respect of a particular part of the general theory : it deals with the relation between disordered thought and speech in the insane as seen from Blondel's own point of view. It first appeared, in substance, as the chapter entitled *La Pensée Morbide et le Langage*, in the larger work already mentioned. The enquiring student will, however, find other studies indicated in the short list given at the end of this note of introduction.

Blondel's general theory of the Insane Mind, as is made clear by his own *apologia*, came into being under the twin, yet unlike influences of Durkheim and of Bergson. He derived from the first writer his notions of the effect exercised by the social environment upon the individual modalities of consciousness. But it is the second who taught him the importance of Speech, or Language, in shaping the mind of the Individual.

INTRODUCTION

Struck, in the course of his clinical observations upon the insane, by the grossly obvious contradiction between the verbal assertions and the behaviour of those subjects whose personalities are disturbed, he came to feel that some inward coherence, some logical arrangement unable to find expression within the confines of the accustomed linguistic conventions known to the patients, lies behind the incoherence and exuberance of the unintelligible verbigeration with which they confound our understanding.

His point of view thus became one which may be facetiously compared to that of the exasperated telephone subscriber who, in final despair, begged the operator at the Exchange to tell him for which number he should ask in order to get connection with that which he desired! The same grasp of an essential situation was displayed by the countryman who found no difficulties—so he averred— in understanding the vagaries of his timepiece, declaring that, when the hands stood at twenty to six, and it struck half past four, he knew it was then just eight o'clock. So, perhaps, may we explain the inconsistency of the behaviour and the speech of the insane, with themselves, and with reality.

At any rate—to give his theory in the simplest terms—Blondel, rejecting all attempts at explanation of this contrast or inconsistency which assume some basis in perceptive experience for the verbal affirmations, came to believe that, for persons of the kind now under consideration, language has become dislocated from its normal functioning. A 'number' being asked for which is not on the switchboard, the operator connects the caller with one that is useless to him—unless, by happy chance, it proves to be the one the caller really wanted but, by his own fault, did not 'give correctly'!

For Blondel, healthily working minds welcome only those experiences which are easily identified or classified by their resemblance to the fruits of 'collective experience' and which find at hand, suitable 'ready-for-service' linguistic forms. What in our individual experience, our feelings, our thoughts, is most personal, is generally repulsed into the subconsciousness as irreducible to the symbolic verbal formulae provided by social experience.

But nothing is more personal to each one of us than is the cenesthesia, that sum of inner sensation or *sentiment* which is now so generally attributed to the visceral mass, in connection with the sympathetic—as opposed to the cerebro-spinal—nervous system.

Normally, and for the normal person, cenesthesia remains, in Blondel's phrase, on the outskirts of the consciousness, or mind, since it has no appropriate linguistic expression; for the reasons just given. It may, however, be observed, in parenthesis—and the point is perhaps not altogether unimportant—that in those few moments when consciousness of all the external world other than some very immediate "object" is almost in abeyance, and organic life is almost wholly given over to direction by the vegetable, or sympathetic nervous system, cenesthesia attains an overwhelming intensity and finds linguistic expression—of a kind, it is true—onomatopoeic, and primitive, but still linguistic—that cannot be denied utterance.

But when *repressed* cenesthesia persistently invades the sphere of normal consciousness, as, according to Blondel's hypothesis, is the case for the insane mind, then the patient, trying to express what he feels, finds his experience beyond the resources of his habitual linguistic reserve, and the cenesthesia taking on—as if by *force majeure*—some disorderly verbal expression, he becomes conscious of the antagonism between his experiences and the seized verbal symbolisms, and suffers from those feelings of disintegration, disorder, and alienation that emotionally characterize the insane mind.

Hence, too, since the cenesthesia cannot fully satisfy itself symbolically within the limitations of the available verbal paradigms, are given the characteristics of the speech and utterances of these patients.

This, in barest outline, is Blondel's theory of the insane mind, of *la conscience morbide*; in distinction to the healthy, normal mind, or *conscience claire*. Its appreciation depends to some extent upon acquaintance with the insane—as distinguished from the merely neurotic, or hysterical. (Blondel is an alienist *de carrière,* and not a pathological neurologist or a literary psychologist.) It depends, too, upon the degree of assent given to the notion of the cenesthesia as constituted by " inner sensations " which, not being connected with external objects through sense organs, cannot give rise to corresponding verbal or other concepts with symbolic expressions, and remain, so to speak, the exclusive property of the individual—never being susceptible of objective investigation.

A difficulty which should not be a difficulty, and which does however give rise to some interesting lines of thought, is brought about by Blondel's persistent use of the French word *conscience* (in the terms *conscience claire,* and *conscience morbide*) when he refers to sums of states of consciousness, or to *Mind,* sane or insane, sound or disordered. Every schoolgirl, of course, knows that the French word *conscience* means, on different occasions (i)consciousness (ii)conscientiousness and (iii) conscience ; the sentiment of our being : the quality of being scrupulously careful in the performance of duty : and the sentiment of the difference between good and evil, respectively. We know too, that, as Lord Morley somewhere observes, for a Frenchman *conscience* (in the English sense) is a matter of right and wrong in the sphere of intellect rather than, as for an Englishman, in the sphere of morality, or ethics. But still, Blondel's theory must have interest for theological and other moralists since it affords them the opportunity to identify the struggle between the fruits of social experience and cenesthesia with the struggle between good and evil, or between conscience and self-love. They may point out that the " troubled conscience " *does* follow conflict between two urges or tendencies, whereof the one resents and revolts against the repression, or repulsion, exercised against it by the pressure of social experience. It matters very little whether when we employ the word *conscience* in the ordinary English way we are considering it as the result of collective or social experience carried (if the simile be permitted) to capital account and available when required, or whether we follow Kant in considering it as the result of Reason guiding the Practical Life. But we may point out that, while Stekel now constantly explains conflict in the mental sphere as due to clash between Conscience and Repressed Desire (the latter resisting Repression) so Butler, in his famous *First Sermon* lays it down that we were made for society and to promote the happiness thereof just as we are intended to take care of our own life and health and private good; thus (as a competent critic has said) reducing the authorities in the polity of the soul to two: self-love and conscience. When these two are in harmonious co-operation the tranquil mind carries on its functions and gives verbal or other motor expression to its contents: when there is conflict, the "troubled conscience" is betrayed by inconsistencies in speech and in behaviour.

So, after all, there may be fundamentally something more in common between the eighteenth-century Anglican bishop and the twentieth-century psychologist at Strasbourg than an academician would —very properly—be disposed to allow. In fact, to use the terminology of Messrs. Ogden and Richards (in the *Meaning of Meaning*) two observers remote in time and space, each subservient to special social experiences and languages, while observing the same sets of *referents*, have come to construct vastly differing *references* and yet, ultimately, to approximate very closely in matter of verbal *symbolization*.

But, after all, no one now-a-days seeks more than this from any general theory: that it should be convenient; convenient as a *résumé* of facts, otherwise less conveniently resumed; convenient also as a starting-point from which observation, confirmatory or contradictory, but in any case useful and again convenient, may be made. And so Blondel's theory requires, and will obtain, discussion and analysis, not only for what it is in itself, but in comparison with those of Bleuler, Janet, Freud, and half a score more. In this way, by comparison of rival theories, in the fashion that Masson-Oursel has taught us, in his *Comparative Philosophy*, we shall better attain a just, even though temporarily inexpressible, notion about the data in question.

Each of the theories now before the psychological world affords us a method of classifying our clinical cases and of constructing, for didactic and clinical purposes if we will, forms of mental alienation or 'clinical entities'. Each method employs as the index what each author holds to be the dominating psychological phenomenon. For Freud this is, perhaps, the lowering of the censorship: for Bleuler, loss of contact with reality: for Janet, loss of the function of the real; for Blondel, the rise of cenesthenia into consciousness. And so on.

All this has been particularly well set out, by Villey-Desméserets, in a valuable essay (Paris, 1924. Jouve et cie.) wherein he echoes Chaslin in saying that it is not so much our duty to accept or reject any one of these rival theories as to study each one under its own *angle de valeur*, passing all through the sieve of our own logic so that none of them hinders us from 'seeing the facts.'

Indeed, the importance of psychological theories is such that they form an integral part of psychology—a science which has a logic and a value quite other than those of the experimental sciences and which, while none the less than they a science, is one for which the "experimental facts" *are* these very general theories put forward in explanation of the observations made in clinical medicine and in daily life. That is to say: these theories are the experimental facts of psychology; the testing of them by reference to clinical facts constitutes the experiment, as truly as does observation upon a frog constitute a "fact" of scientific medicine.

And so, Villey-Desméserets has had the happy idea of reducing some of these theories—those of Janet, Bleuler, Freud and Blondel—to terms of physiology, and of expressing each in turn, schematically and diagrammatically, as a form or variety of physiological reflex action.

On pages 20 and 21 are given two diagrams —adapted and modified from Villey-Desméserets—showing in this fashion the notions of (i) *la conscience claire* and (ii) *la conscience morbide.* It is hoped that these diagrams are self-explanatory, but, at the risk of repetition, it may be said that we suppose a state of clear conscience to be provoked by a sensation—the result of an object of experience—coming into relation with an appropriate referent, or concept, which, formed as the consequence of social experience, has an appropriate verbal or motor outcome or linguistic or other symbol, called into expression by the state of ' clear consciousness '. Cenesthesia remains on the outskirts of the clear consciousness; the mind is untroubled; no linguistic or behaviouristic incongruity is observed. The mind is sane.

But the diagram schematic of the *conscience morbide* represents cenesthesia as impinging upon the consciousness; striving for identification with *some* concept present to that consciousness in order that it may possess itself of some

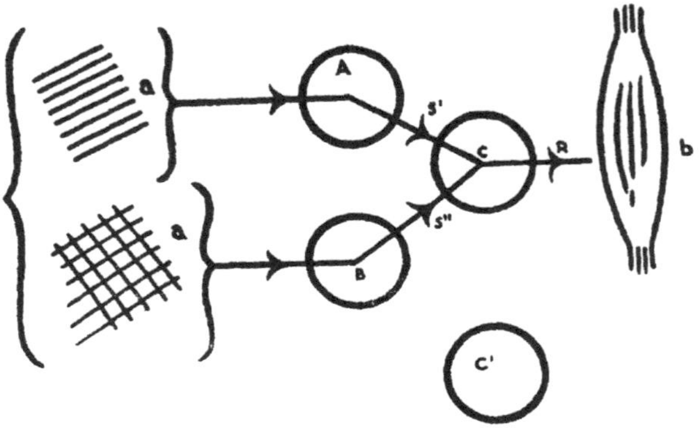

PLATE I.

La Conscience Claire

(*after* Villey-Desméserets)

a External Object of Experience.

b Motor Expression.

A Sensation.

B Concept derived from Experience (Collective).

S', S" Excitatory and Tonic Affluents.

C LA CONSCIENCE CLAIRE.

C' Cenesthesia.

R Motor Effluents.

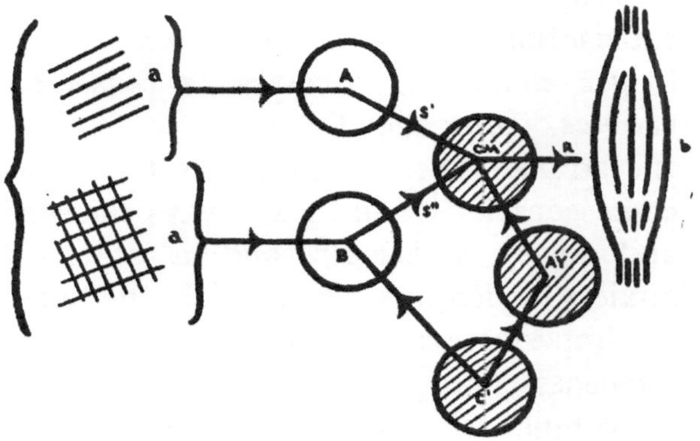

PLATE II.

La Conscience Morbide

(*after* Villey-Desméserets).

a	External Object of Experience.
b	Motor Expression.
A	Sensation.
B	Concept derived from Experience (Collective).
S′, S″	Excitatory and Tonic Affluents.
CM	LA CONSCIENCE MORBIDE.
AY	Anxiety State.
C′	Cenesthesia.
R	Motor Effluents.

linguistic or other means of expression, so relieving tension and bringing about satisfaction. So *la conscience* is no longer *claire*; it becomes *la conscience morbide*, embracing three components;—the strange, unrecognized cenesthesia become conscious; an idea always renewed and never satisfied; and a state of anxiety which, arising through the sense of imperfection in the troubled consciousness is, psychologically, of great importance although, physiologically, of feeble tension.

The student may, if he will, construct easily for himself analogous diagrams illustrative of any of those theories that interest him. But the psychopathological theory that will ultimately hold sway must satisfy two functions. It must 'explain' or cover the greatest number of facts that are usefully covered, at the same time that it leaves uncovered the greatest number of such facts that can usefully be left 'unexplained'. But the usefulness or relevancy of those selected to be covered or explained, and the uselessness or irrelevancy of those left on one side, can only be determined by reference to what is 'the case' for the particular observer at a particular moment. In the words of Wittgenstein, in his *Tractatus Logico-Philosophicus*,

'Die Welt ist alles, was der Fall ist.'

* * * *

Blondel's work must now speak for itself. But perhaps the chief interest in it for the present writer lies in this, that some twenty-five years ago, when writing upon the study of insanity, in an essay afterwards reprinted (*Essays and Clinical Studies*, 1911) he ventured to draw attention to the rise into consciousness, during insane dissolution of mind, of that component of mind then called subject-consciousness, but now clearly identifiable with Blondel's cenesthesia, as well as to maintain, with Sankey, that all insanities begin with a stage of 'melancholy,' no less clearly identifiable with the necessary, even if transitory anxiety stage that Blondel finds to obtain whenever *la conscience claire* passes into *la conscience morbide.*

And Blondel's theory is one which attempts to explain in terms of psychology that which the present writer tried to explain in terms of physiology, in an earlier paper, on the Physical Signs of Insanity (*loc. cit.*) : ' the apparent dislocation of expression and emotion in insanity .'

F. G. CROOKSHANK.

London, W.
1928.

SELECT BIBLIOGRAPHY

I. *La Conscience Morbide.* Paris, 1914. 1928².

II. La documentation psychiatrique dans l'Intelligence de Taine. *Congrès de Philosophie,* 1921.

III. La Conscience Morbide. *Journal de Psychologie,* 1923, pp. 128-146.

IV. *La Psychanalyse.* Paris, 1924.

V. Le Langage et la Pensée chez l'enfant. *Revue d'Histoire et de Philosophie religieuses,* 1924, v. pp. 456-480.

VI. Psychologie Pathologique et Sociologie, *Journal de Psychologie,* 1925, pp. 326-359.

VII. La Personnalité. Les Volitions. *Traité de Psychologie,* par Dumas (T. II, ch. ii., ch. v.)

VIII. *Introduction à la Psychologie Collective.* Paris, 1928.

I.

THE INSANE MIND

I have chosen the insane mind as the subject of this essay, because I shall then be able to deal with the system of ideas which has drawn most attention to my work. It has seemed to me that what would be most interesting to those who do not know that work would be to learn what are the really essential elements in the ideas which I have put forward, while I hope to satisfy a certain curiosity in others by discussing that work. Such an essay as this is fortunately confined within certain natural limits. Its relative brevity forces one to ignore details, to leave out connecting links, and thus to bring out the more clearly the strength or weakness of the whole structure of ideas dealt with.

I shall, therefore, outline the genesis of those ideas which I have expressed in *La Conscience Morbide*. Egoism is detestable no doubt. But we psychologists are obliged by the nature of our calling to treat it with a little indulgence, and to tell the story of one's thought is often an act of humility rather than one of arrogance. All of which amounts to saying that I owe more to the teachers who have influenced me, and to the facts which I have observed, than I do to my own efforts !

Somewhere about 1900, when I was beginning my medical studies, two movements upon which I wish for the moment to focus your attention, were among many others, developing in the world of French thought. I mean the movements led by Durkheim, and by Bergson.

It is not my intention to expound the ideas of Durkheim. Only one point need now occupy our attention, to wit : the peculiar importance of sociology for psychology owing to the tendency of the former to supplant the latter. One of the cardinal points in Durkheim's teaching is that though physiological phenomena may not explain those psychological, the psychological fail equally to explain collective phenomena. The social group is something more than the sum of the individuals which compose it. It lives its own life, dominating the individual by its conditions and its laws. Its being expresses itself in the individual mind, so to speak, by systems of ideas, rules, and imperatives which were not there brought to birth at the mere instigation of the environment in which this individual (mind) moves, but came to it ready-made and with all the rigidity imparted to them by the universalization of the group. Moral, religious and social conceptions, institutions, and legal rights, are not the result of the more or less concerted co-operation of individuals, but are imposed upon them by the group.

As a result, psychology is, by itself, unable to give a complete account of the development of individual minds. Mental life in its highest form belongs to the realm of sociology. Between lower and higher, simple and complex, it is no longer merely a question of the difference between the methods used for their study, but of a difference of kind. Collective representations—to speak the language of sociology—ideas which the individual is incapable of creating by himself, which are imposed upon him from the outside, which inspire him with fear, love or respect—all these are social things. The more Durkheim's work developed, the wider grew the realm of these collective representations which were thus withdrawn from the realm of psychology. Durkheim, no doubt, admits that organic changes, sensations, perceptions, and elementary emotions are of a psychological nature. But in his last book the laws of logic, categories, and concepts, the whole system of knowledge and action, of intelligence and reason, take on a social character; so that there is, so to speak, no corner of psychological life left which is not filled with collective representations.

Finally, Lévy-Bruhl has shown that it is impossible to reproduce in our own minds the thoughts of primitive races because the whole life of these people is scored from one end to another by collective influences. Not only can their higher mental manifestations—

knowledge, religion, ethics, art—be neither compared nor in any way reduced to ours, but primitive peoples do not feel, sense, perceive or imagine in a manner in any way resembling ours. At this point psychology gives the impression of having been practically routed from its own domain, and of being in the last resort reduced to psycho-physics and to psycho-physiology. Given the stimulus and the immediate psychological repercussion, the conscious sequel will be determined by laws acting from without. Society does not create man, does not endow him with intellect. But his potential intellect becomes dynamic and concrete only as a function of the society of which he is a part. Similarly, with regard to consciousness as a whole, it is society which informs it and enables it to pass from a state of potentiality to one of action.

All this is rather disturbing news for psychologists. It becomes more disturbing still if we bring it into line with another claim made from an opposite pole of contemporary thought by a metaphysical system standing out in bold defiance of all our accustomed habits of thought. It will be sufficient for me to stress one element only—an essential one it is true—in Bergson's thought. According to Bergson, the light of clear consciousness does not enable us to grasp immediate psychological reality. The latter underlies the former. "Clear consciousness" only presents to us psychological reality fundamentally modified in its structure by practical necessities, by intelligence, language, and by society. Their converging pressure introduces into consciousness a rigidity which imitates matter and is essential to life, but which is repugnant to the essential nature of psychological being.

Bergson holds that Consciousness or Mind which can be broken up into elements according to mechanical laws of thought, which can be divided into states according to the established articulations of language is a socialized consciousness or mind, happily adapted to the necessities of practical life, but no longer marked by immediacy. Bergson's ideas are no doubt metaphysical. But his metaphysics is permeated by a sound and ingenious psychology, which has been put to the test and not found wanting. Ten years before Pierre Marie as clinician and pathological anatomist brought about that great revolution in the domain of aphasia, as early as 1896, Bergson—thus splendidly vindicating the much abused psychology of reflection—Bergson refused to give credence to the then classical theories of aphasia. A precedent this, which undoubtedly gives food for thought!

Be that as it may, the important point for us is that these two great movements of thought, opposed though they were in origin, in tendency, and in spirit, yet contrived to meet at least at one point. For very different reasons and with widely diverging aims, they not only made psychologists aware of the influence exercised upon the play of mind by society and language, but urged them to draw their own conclusions from these findings.

To come back to myself and my work,

however, after this digression which we have found imposed upon us. In 1906, having finished with examinations and candidatures, I devoted myself exclusively to mental diseases, working at the Salpêtrière under the direction of my revered teacher, Dr. Deny. Open-minded, independent, ever on the look-out for new ideas, he was one of the first in France to welcome the theories of Kraepelin, and to introduce them into his books and teaching. I lay stress on this merely to show how unwilling were those, among whom I worked so long, to rest on the discoveries of the past, and how ready were they to realize anew each day the always virgin freshness of the problems which confronted them. It was under this propitious discipline that I first began to examine the insane. Let me state quite shortly the method which I used in my observations. In the friendly converse by means of which I ough to penetrate into patients' minds, I avoided, as far as in me lay, anything that might resemble cross-questioning; I let them speak without interruption, convinced that the fewer and the more discreet my questions, the more likely were the patients to yield up the secret of their ill in all its nakedness. In this way I studied cases for whole months and years together. I used also frequently to take up my stand in the corner of some room or courtyard, and there spend many hours watching patients living and acting according to their own devices. Thus I slowly acquired a cumulative experience, indispensable as I believe to the understanding of insanity.

My curiosity was very soon attracted by those patients who, without suffering any diminution of their intellectual powers, properly so-called, were yet to be recognized, whether plainly delirious or not, by the *anxiety* which accompanied the development of their trouble. But the more deeply I studied these cases, the less I understood them, for they seemed to me incomparable to any others. I could see no way of connecting their way of thinking with ours, nor of reaching a direct understanding of their trouble. Let us take an example, if you like—

the depersonalized subject. These persons, as you know, believe that everything in them has changed, that they no longer possess the intelligence, the activity and the sensibility which once were theirs. Or again, they no longer feel their body in the same way; it no longer has the same suppleness, the same vigour, the same beauty. In the last resort, they cease to be anything at all; they no longer have body, sensations, will, intelligence; they no longer exist *morally*.

In the same way, too, the external world appears to many of these patients as strangely altered, if not actually annihilated. Their symptoms—moral depersonalization, physical depersonalization, strangeness or annihilation of the external world—may each appear in independence of any other but may be combined in the most varied ways. Well, in many of these cases one bald fact always obtruded itself on my notice. The patients complained of complete physical or moral insensibility; yet, the very next moment, if not indeed the very same moment, they would lament, in frenzied accents the enormity of their sufferings or spend themselves in bewailing their fate, in this way not merely miming their own despair, but voicing moral or physical anguish from the very depths of their being! I could see no means of reconciling this insensibility and these indubitable sufferings.

Moreover, the same sort of unintelligibility reigned in their language, which was frequently made up of an accumulation of metaphors; sometimes understood as such, sometimes taken literally. Strictly speaking, I succeeded in understanding their utterances only on the condition of these being isolated from one another. Taking them *en masse*, however, as they were given, I was confronted by a monstrous collection of deformed and hypertrophied concepts, of disconcerting contradictions bluntly put forward, from which the patient could not detach himself, even at the moment when they came within his conscious grasp. At the same time I felt very strongly that behind this logical and verbal incoherence there was an internal and intimate coherence which by an unexpected miracle burst asunder the customary bonds of our thought as soon as it tried to find expression.

I was non-plussed by these patients, and no less so by the theories proposed for the explanation of their troubles, for these did not seem to correspond to the complexity of the real facts.

By their ingenious diversity, the cenesthetic theories, translating as they did the more or less delirious negativisms of the patients into anatomico-physiological language, invited me to regard the morbid disturbances as the outcome of inhibition in the cenesthetic centres, of paralysis in the fibres of association. In such circumstances, of course, the impressions of the moment would no longer produce in the patient those physiological processes which enable them to be integrated in his conscious experience. And then, according to the associational tracts that were reached, according to the cenesthetic areas that were touched, their would ensue depersonalization, physical or mental, or strangeness of the external world. These theories did not satisfy me in any way. In the first place, they seemed to me to be simply explaining the incomprehensible by the unknown. I plead guilty to a certain perverseness of spirit. When people talk to me about centres and fibres, I like them to tell me where these are and also why and how their existence and situation have been ascertained.

In the second place, these theories ran counter to current observation. The fact is that (to say nothing of our own experience of cenesthetic perturbations in organic pain) tabes, with its analgesia, its anesthesia, its hypo-anesthesia, its hyperesthesia and pains of all kinds does not normally bring about mental trouble. In the patients with whom we are concerned, on the other hand, cenesthetic disturbances are either absent, or if they exist present no necessary connexion with the morbid convictions. Since, then, the most obvious cenesthetic modifications do not necessarily bring about mental trouble, why should we, in the presence of such ills, appeal to some modification in cenesthesia (of whatever order we may suppose it to be) when examination fails otherwise to reveal its existence? Even supposing that there are cenesthetic disturbances, what matters most (since they can exist without any concomitant psychical disturbance) is not the cenesthetic disturbance itself, but the manner in which it is experienced; in a word, the mental state of the patient, which is the very question to be explained. Let us then agree to these theories. Let us place at the root of the mental disturbance an inhibition of the cenesthetic centres and their associative tracts. This explains moral insensibility and physical insensibility. But how shall we explain the patients' moments of despair and suffering, since, according to those very physiological theories, these presuppose not only a cenesthesia left intact, but even a sort of cenesthetic erethism?

Psychological theories, on the other hand—such for instance as those of Pierre Janet—did not seem to me to meet the difficulties of the case any better. Janet also took as his starting point those of the patients' utterances which could be regarded as objectively established. The patient would complain of a feeling of incompleteness. This feeling was justified; it corresponded to a definite loss of the function of reality, to a definite slackening of mental tension. Thus the patient was, as he said, really changed; his mental powers were really diminished. I was again puzzled. The patient's psychic activity certainly led to nothing useful or practical, it had certainly lost all or part of its social value; but although this psychic capital was spent in emotional display, in broodings and in gesticulations, it was none the less *spent*, and spent to what seemed to me a considerable degree. I had difficulty in admitting any diminution, if not in the patient's utilizable strength, at any rate in his mental dynamism. Janet's theory, therefore, seemed to me at fault, omitting as it did, for the credit of some of the patients' utterances, to take account of that kind of mental activity betrayed by quite another set of their manifestations.

But all these theories, physiological

and psychological, seemed to me objectionable for precisely the reason that they were based upon the very utterances of the patients, of which I for my part could make neither head nor tail, and which even in their simplest forms I could always indistinctly divine as deliriant. In a word, I felt that it was impossible to give the whole or part of what was said by the patients as an immediate basis for pathogenic interpretation of these cases. Since their speech had ceased to be language, and was no longer fulfilling the two main functions of language. It was no longer language, since it did not enable them to make themselves understood ; it was no longer language, since it served no better to explain to the patients themselves their own conditions.

At times, starting from some mystery which they wished to clear up, the patients after brooding, indulgence in metaphors and rambling incoherences would find themselves in the end confronted with the same mystery. On other occasions when the rambling incoherencies developed into delirium proper, they could not be made to connect with one another and would end by veiling the mystery without removing it ; as when a patient would more or less confusedly think out a new setting to fit a new experience, without, however, feeling any satisfaction in the attempt. Morbid thought thus showed itself foreign to ours and foreign to its own part, since it was unable, in order to be clear to itself and to others, to make use of the language which till then had served that purpose.

Thus it was in trying to find out about morbid mentality I came to ask myself—of course as a psychologist, not a linguist—what relation existed between normal consciousness and language, and through this unexpected excursion into pathology to link up the sociological and the Bergsonian trends of thought. Since we do not understand these patients ; since they do not understand themselves ; what is the peculiar process in our minds which enables us to understand ourselves and to make ourselves understood by others ? At this point two considerations of the utmost importance led me to take fuller cognizance of a cardinal fact which can, I believe, throw more light on the problem of the insane mind.

In the first place, we do not create our language. To an immense extent we receive it ready-made from the group of which we are a part. The system of ideas and the logical organization incorporated in language are imposed upon our thought from without. Language brings into our thought a clarity, a distinctiveness, and a generality, which outrun the fruit of individual experience, even if we suppose the latter capable by its own means of achieving such a result. And language does not espouse natural and universal forms of thought. There are diverse types of language, and between contemporary tongues there are undeniable differences in the manner in which ideas are disposed, ordered, and subordinated to each other. Consequently, though one would never have suspected it without reflecting upon the matter, the form which our thought receives from our language is not that which it would have taken if we had been born in another country.

One and the same individual consciousness is therefore susceptible, according to the language it uses, of developing towards itself and towards others, according to a plan which is not identical with itself in all times and in all places. Moreover, this effect upon us of the place where we live is not confined to the imposition of our language upon us. It regulates our miming and our actions. We do not only learn to speak, we learn to feel, and to do, in accordance with certain models of emotion and action. To depart from these models is to commit blunders, faults, even crimes. It is at any rate running the risk of misleading others as to what our feelings and intentions really are. Language, in fact, has supplied to us, written down in its own terms, a system of ready-made concepts and their relations of reciprocal subordination. Here, the collective group furnishes us with a system of mimetic expressions and ready-made actions generally applicable to cases of the same order; we may even say, if a certain stretch of terminology be permitted, with a sytem of mimetic and motor concepts.

On the other hand—and this is our second consideration—unreflective thought spontaneously and naturally embodies Bain's formula, that to think is to abstain from talking and acting. In other words, we express to ourselves internally the manifestations of our conscious activity in the same way that we translate them into words and objective actions for others. And this internal action and internal speech seem to us quite adequate for our thought. Once this potential action and speech stands out clearly in our minds, we feel that we have completely mastered the contents of our consciousness. All psychological analysis is, in a sense, verbal analysis which, with the ostensible object of fixing our thought, exposes it in its inmost essence to an increasing permeation by linguistic abstractions.

If this is really so, then clear consciousness—the healthy mind—in which normal thought finds satisfaction and balance—presents a truly singular character. Over and above our private conceptions, our individual experience, resting on the wide basis of collective experience, establishes the notion of homogeneous space, in which the objects so perceived are placed no longer as the mere objects of our personal perception but as the objects of all possible perceptions, necessary and valid for others as well as for ourselves. In the same way, over and above our strictly individual mental happenings there arises with the help of language and through its incessant activity the plan of what we may call homogeneous consciousness, in which our mental life breaks up distinct elements which are interchangeable between one mind and another. For you to understand me when I talk about my pain, my joy, my sadness—the most private events of my life; for me to share in this understanding; language must isolate what is common to your mental states and to mine, and there must have been thus constituted a sort of common consciousness in which our individual minds can meet and recognize each other. Consequently, the effect of language is, from this point of view, to objectify and generalize the facts of private consciousness, just as the effect of the notion of space is to objectify and generalize the world of our sensations. But in these conditions, normal consciousness, in which normal thought makes sure of itself and feels at home, is an impersonal consciousness. Since, then, the mental events of no two people can be absolutely identical, and since language, which stabilizes the dimly outlined distinctions inside the individual consciousness, essentially varies from one social group to another, and from one epoch to another, our thought, in order to ripen in the full sun of clear consciousness, must needs on the way rid itself all that makes it properly and irreducibly ours.

Thus the characteristic of normal consciousness is to develop according to the laws marked out by language within the framework constituted by mimetic and motor concepts, to place itself in the plan of the common homogeneous consciousness, and there to find itself at home. But this subordination of our individual states to concepts of all kinds is possible only by eliminating from these states everything that makes them individual. Normal consciousness therefore, in order thus to find its place in the plan of common consciousness, must also have the characteristic of turning away from all its irreducibly individual elements which, by persistently imposing themselves, would necessarily block its progress towards generality and intelligibility. To itself, normal consciousness appears to be clear consciousness; and clear consciousness is that in which, while we are telling ourselves or others the contents of our thought, whatever cannot be spoken within the limits of language or acted according to motor concepts can find no place and is therefore eliminated.

Upon what, then, in the main, is directed this elimination which turns individual consciousness into clear consciousness, *i.e.*, something capable of moving about without effort inside the plan mapped out for human activity by language and intelligence? Of all the objects of our experience there is one which remains irreducibly the contents of an exclusively individual experience. The external perception of every object but this is common and shared by all men. But with regard to our own body we are forever imprisoned within our private experience. For the external senses (but for those alone) it is, no doubt, an object of experience on a par with others, both for ourselves and for other people. But nothing of all that reaches our consciousness from the depths of our internal organs is ever felt by any but ourselves. Our experience of it is never confronted by any other experience. Cenesthesia, to which we have thus been led back, is perhaps the unique type of strictly individual experience. And this cenesthesia, be it said at once. must be regarded as it is experienced. Consequently, it must not, from the psychological point of view, be considered as a sum of hypothetical organic sensations of whose individual and isolated existence we have no direct experience. For normally cenesthesia is felt, or rather lived, as an indistinct mass underlying

clear consciousness and its doings. The dim feeling of its presence suffices for clear consciousness, which then turns its attention and its efforts in other directions.

The history of ideas indicates that this really is so. It was not until the nineteenth century that cenesthesia was, so to speak, discovered, and that neurological and psychiatric research came to a full realization of its importance. Would it not have been otherwise if clear consciousness had not always turned away from the subject? Be it noted, moreover, that even when such and such a pain and such and such a feeling of discomfort stands out more acutely from the cenesthetic mass, it is only by a series of artifices that we can form any idea of it. We localize it; we compare it to such and such a sensory impression as a prick, a burn, or a feeling of pressure; we enquire into its causes, we are anxious about its effects. We therefore incorporate it into a system of ideas borrowed from our objective experience, and it is only in a roundabout manner that we contrive to realize it and describe it. We are satisfied with this notation. And yet it only circumscribes our pain without representing it! Without this notation we could say nothing about the pain, and even with it there remains something which cannot be expressed. But—and this is the essential point—the normal individual is not concerned about what this inexpressible element in his pain may be. He is anxious about it, no doubt, but he is apprehensive of the effects which the experience of his group has led him to fear, and his curiosity is not directed on to the fundamental nature of his pain, on to its affective substance, so to speak. From the mere fact that he has fixed it in an objective setting it is known and familiar in his eyes. You may perhaps have guessed the reason for this. Clear consciousness, or normal consciousness, is that which communes with itself and with others. Now, cenesthesia does not commune with itself, for language is the fruit of collective experience, and cenesthesia and collective experience contradict one another. Thus, in the normal mind, the underlying cenesthesia carries clear consciousness, and clear consciousness allows itself to be carried by cenesthesia without attempting to know it otherwise than in a roundabout way.

But from the psychological point of view cenesthesia, however original and peculiar the manner in which we apprehend it, has the same claim to psychic reality as clear consciousness. It is therefore the duty of psychology to conceive a total consciousness comprising both cenesthesia and clear consciousness. For, from the depths of cenesthesia, and under influences which transcend it, clear consciousness emerges to the surface, there to spread itself out in all its discrete complexity, commensurable with language; while the cenesthetic mass sinks down to the lower stratum where it vegetates, in the full sense of the term—confused, veiled and almost unnoticed. Of this total consciousness we gain a fleeting experience which the normal individual is always ready to correct and dismiss, when, falling back as it were upon our own essence and feeling the original and irrevocable rhythm of our organic life, we realize that the objects we see, the events which happen to us, the emotions we feel, and the thoughts we cherish are coloured in a unique and incomparable manner by all that we at that moment are, and that consequently they can never be twice the same. But objects, events, feelings, and unique ideas are the stuff neither of intelligence nor of action. And that is why, in order to understand and to act, we turn away from what constitutes these objects, these feelings, and these unique mental states.

We try to defend ourselves against cenesthetic influences by " coming back amongst men " as Amiel puts it ; that is to say, by placing ourselves once more in the realm of clear consciousness, where the mystery and melancholy of the unique fade away in the light of the universal. We are thus led to admit that for the creation of normal consciousness a certain separation akin to the pouring off of one liquid from another must take place within the total consciousness. In this way elements common to all minds, capable of being expressed in words defined by collective experience and translated into actions regulated by the group, rise into full consciousness and display themselves there. They are practically freed from any adherence to the cenesthetic mass which in the meantime settles down into the subconscious where, lived rather than felt or known, it finds its normal seat.

This interpretation of normal consciousness is certainly incomplete and perhaps incorrect. But at any rate I hope I have awakened you to the reality of the following problem of which it offers a solution. Given the necessary character of language, how is it that the individual mind can bend itself to verbal forms and so utterly mistake their very nature as to actually identify itself with them? Now this is the very problem which we must solve if we wish to understand morbid consciousness. For, since the language of the insane is unintelligible to us, it must be because the insane mind is in rebellion against the conceptual system utilized by normal consciousness. And the crux of the problem we have set ourselves is, after all, to know what it is that does or does not happen in the unsound mind which does not or does happen in the sound mind, and which prevents the former from submitting to the limitations set by the group with the ease and spontaneity brought to the task by the latter. My conception may therefore be rejected, in any case it will have to be completed ; but—and this in my view is the essential point—the problem itself cannot be denied.

Before going any further I must needs ask you to agree with me for a moment that my hypothesis is well founded ; that our total consciousness is really what I have just told you ; and that within this total consciousness (by means of the separation there effected through the triple operation of intelligence, society, and language) the normal mind, absorbed so to speak in the collective unfolding of clear consciousness, turns away from the dimly moving cenesthetic mass on which it rests as on a continuous and mobile foundation. Supposing that through psychological or physiological processes of whose precise nature we are ignorant —since, when all is said and done, we are always, alas! thrown back upon the intervention of more or less latent predispositions—supposing, then, that this separation is rendered impossible, and supposing consequently that the elements, destined by the collective urge to proceed freely from the depths of the total consciousness to the realm of clear consciousness, no longer succeed in detaching themselves from the cenesthetic mass and therefore retain about them something ineffably individual: What will happen in these new conditions?

For one thing, it is quite clear that the mind will no longer be able to move about on the plan traced out by the group; each effort which it makes to release its elements from the total consciousness will meet with a secret inner resistance on their part due to the cenesthetic mass to which they are still bound. This fact alone will mean that the mind is departing from normality and entering upon the morbid. In the second place, the mind disturbed in this way will remain full of the memories of its normal state and of the manner in which it previously took cognizance of itself. It will therefore feel lost in this new psychological environment where, for lack of the reductions previously performed with unconscious spontaneity, its various states will no longer wear its former aspect—that aspect which has become so familiar and natural that it seemed to seize and reflect the mind's very essence and the totality of its being.

The patient, no doubt, will still find himself able both to speak and to handle mimetic and motor concepts and *because* of this power his psychological activity will be manifested in verbal and motor expressions. But from the fact that the separation of the individual and the cenesthetic has ceased to operate, the mind, when it unfolds itself in verbal and motor expressions (whether these are directed to the outer world or are maintained inside consciousness so as to fix it on itself) can no longer cover the psychological entities which were once at its command. For these are now rebellious to the former generalization, to that translation into anonymous terms which is the very essence of clear consciousness and the normal mind. The patient can no longer recognize his own mental states in the terms which he uses to describe them to himself, nor in the movements which he outlines in imagination. He loses himself in futile search for a discursive system which would be more closely wedded to the form of his thoughts and feelings and would give him back the peace in which his mind was wont to dwell.

All this gives rise in the patient to a terrifying question as to the nature of these states of consciousness so like his former ones, and yet so different. For this difference is of a kind never before met with. It can be neither defined nor expressed; in a word, it cannot melt into that very definition and form of expression which by connecting it with earlier experience would do away with its mysterious character. At this stage the patient becomes absorbed in the mystery which enshrouds his conscious life and in the anxiety which it causes him to feel. The existence of this stage of mystification and anxiety is not suggested to us by the requirements of our theme, but all the classical descriptions of systematized delirium agree in pointing out an initial period of anxiety which is the forerunner of delirium properly so-called.

Moreover, this mystification and this anxiety are general because the disturbance is everywhere, and the cenesthetic invasion takes place simultaneously at every point of consciousness. But the process by which the normal mind takes cognizance of itself continues willy-nilly to persist in the morbid mind, and to try and distinguish amongst its various elements and states. The disease thus becomes a sort of attribute applied in turn to the perceptions, to the representations, to the feelings, and to the ideas amongst which successively the morbid mind attempts to distribute itself. It tends to find an objective expression in delirious utterances. But as the trouble is everywhere, the delirious urge is carried in every direction at once. Delirium will often, according to conditions and circumstances which vary from one case to another, develop in one direction in preference to all others, and this justifies the clinical distinctions made between, *e.g.*, ideas of guilt, of persecution, of negation, of possession or of megalomania. But on closer inspection we may say that no delirium is ever entirely homogeneous. Observation and analysis will always disclose other deliriums, which are either abortive, arrested in their development, or merely incipient. And between these various deliriums, or rather between the various features of one and the same delirium, we can grasp no other unity than that of the general disturbance of which they are the disconcerting manifestation.

Let us, for the sake of clarity, confine our examination to ideas of strangeness and depersonalization. The patient lives under a double obsession: the obsession of mystery and anxiety which confronts him in the irreducible heterogeneity of his present and past experience ; the obsession of the memory of that clear consciousness in which, in former times, apparently free from impediment, he felt the supple, fertile play of all his mental doings. This state of clear consciousness remains in his eyes the type and standard of conscious life. Compared to it, the change of which he is aware can only be a process of diminution, of degradation and decadence. Things have changed, he cannot see them as before, they are not so clear, so definite, so brilliant ; everything is confused. The world is, therefore, less real to him than it used to be. His body has changed; he no longer feels it as before ; it is not so strong, so supple, so healthy, so beautiful. It is, therefore, less real for him than formerly. His mind and heart have changed ; he has lost his intelligence, his will and his moral sensitiveness. His mind and heart are, therefore, less real to him than they were. But the alteration which has been interpreted in this way remains as mysterious and terrifying as ever. So that in order to express this untranslatable change, the patient actually reaches a stage where he is not content to talk of the world, his body and his self as less real than formerly. He asserts that the world is annihilated, that he himself no longer has a body, that he has lost all capacity for sensation, that he is dead, that he is immortal, that he has lost all power of feeling, all intelligence, all mental activity; that, to tell the truth, he no longer exists. He piles up metaphors and wears himself out in trying to interpret his illness.

For instance, he will conceive his body as in turn diminished, annihilated, dead, or immortal if—insensible thus to the most flagrant contradictions, so crushed beneath the mystery and terror of a change which nothing can render explicable to him—he does not appeal to you at the same moment to consider it with him as both annihilated and immortal. While, finally, the mirage of clear consciousness obliges him to interpret this change as a loss of moral and physical sensibility, given that at the very moment that he is proclaiming his moral and physical insensibility the unimpaired complexity of the patient's consciousness, his obvious distress, his explosions of grief cry out to the observer as a living testimony to the persistence within the sick man's consciousness of all the psycho-motor richness in those affective states whose very existence he denies in his delirium. But even in these so coarsely obvious emotional manifestations the patient, intoxicated so to speak by the irreducible change which has taken place in his mind, no longer recognizes the emotions which he once experienced, he can no longer locate them or understand them. The truth is that only what is intelligible—*i.e.* only what can find its place within the framework which sanctioned by the *group* has fixed into language is humanly real—Whatever obstinately resists expression is equally rebellious to intelligence. And this it is which, before a delirium has attempted to constitute a new experience, even often after it has vainly made this effort—this it is which finds itself eliminated from universal and typical reality as well as from what is intelligible.

The cenesthetic theories are, therefore, in a sense correct. Cenesthesia plays a fundamental part in the genesis of certain mental illnesses. But in order to play this part it has no need to undergo any intrinsic modification. All it need do, all it must do, is to rise in all its obscure presence and restore to the sound mind the indistinctness, the continuity, the irreducible originality of what is purely psychological and essentially individual.

In the same way, Janet is right—in a sense. True, the patient complains of a feeling of incompleteness; true, he has lost the function of reality. But this incompleteness is a delirious idea by whose help he tries to explain the change that has taken place in him; if he has lost the function of reality, it is not that reality actually eludes him, but that he is unable to abstract it from the mental whole in which it nevertheless subsists in entirety. As a matter of fact, the patient seems rather to be suffering from surfeit; psychologically, his consciousness is fuller than normal consciousness, the reality which it embraces is more thickly populated than that apprehended by the normal mind. But this surfeit, this abundance, is ineffectual and dangerous, for it is made up of irreducibly subjective elements whose elimination is a matter of life and death for any man destined to develop in collective surroundings which inform his conscience, his reason and his will.

We have now reached the last link in a long chain of ideas. If I have succeeded in showing you what I owe to the sociological conception of collective representations, to Bergson's speculations and, finally, to the observation of the insane, I shall consider myself satisfied.

To tell the truth, it has been my effort to set about the interpretation of mental disease by a free use of the method employed by Lévy-Bruhl in the study of mental functions in primitive societies. His book has played the most important part in the development of my ideas.

It confirmed me in the direction which my thought first took, and it showed me how it had been possible, in another domain, to triumph over difficulties analogous to those which I was encountering. Just as there can be no question of our re-thinking what was thought by primitive minds, so also must the attempt be given up to re-feel and re-think what is felt and thought by the insane. There is no device by which our minds can identify themselves with states of which the most that can be said is that we have only a dim and elusive experience of them. Here, as there, the task is one of reconstitution and reconstruction. This, then is the conjecture I have made, with the help of the various means which I have put before you, as to the essential difference which we must suppose to exist between the sane and the insane mind, if we may understand what was at first unintelligible to us in the patient's behaviour.

This conception, you may say, is too wide, too general, and cannot explain the detail of delirium. I not only agree, but

E

I will cry it on the house-tops. I meant my conception to be general and to help towards the understanding of a more or less extended group of cases. I have been studying mental disease for some years. When a patient is brought to me I believe myself capable of making both a diagnosis and a prognosis. But I declare myself incapable of explaining a delirium in detail, and above all of explaining it in terms borrowed from our experience, for I have a deep conviction that insane experience is incommensurable with ours. How, for instance, can I say that such and such an event has brought about such and such a mental disturbance? Either the event has been normally felt by the patient, and there is nothing to make us attribute morbid consequences in consciousness to a normally felt event, its results unfolding themselves in a normal way, or the event has been felt in an abnormal manner, in which case it is already an integral part of the morbid disturbance. But it is then not the latter's cause, and we have to find a new explanation of the manner in which it is felt. It

is, therefore, deliberately, and in virtue of that prudence which, I believe, the present state of our knowledge necessitates, that I have given so generalized a conception of the insane mind. Ignorant as I am of the thousand subterfuges which cenesthesia (always at the mercy of countless physiological and psychological circumstances) is capable of using when it rises into the insane mind in the shape of dimly outlined but ever-fading concepts, I have chosen to be silent about them rather than to imagine them in accordance with my own fancy.

II.

INSANE THOUGHT AND LANGUAGE*

The study of intellectual reactions raises many difficulties. We would not, indeed, suggest that affecto-motor and motor reactions give us no clue to the mental state of a patient; but if we are to grasp the extraordinary diversity and detail of such states of mind, the only means which we can use unreservedly, so to speak, is to enter into conversation with our patients, and to take down what they say. Objective examination may lead us to suspect the existence of morbid manifestations of an intellectual order, but the intellectual reactions do not seem definitely and incontestably disturbed until language bears conclusive witness of this trouble, by emphasizing changes of meaning in the ordinary conceptual routine.

Now it is obvious enough that discursive expression possesses a certain

* The names in the following pages refer to cases dealt with in *La Conscience Morbide*.

flexibility which renders it adaptable, at any rate approximately, to a considerable range of mental states ; when, therefore, the limits of this flexibility and approximation are not exceeded, it may preserve a normal appearance but at the same time conceal forms of thought that are in fact pathological. Here is a first indication of the necessity for taking the utmost precaution in our analysis and interpretation of the sayings of patients, even when they appear to talk our language and never express a single aberrant idea, though their affecto-motor and motor reactions have made us suspicious of their mental processes.

This need for precaution will become more evident if we consider that pathological language is sometimes completely incomprehensible to us, and that at these times we must not argue exclusively from cases where we seem to understand it, for the intelligibility is only apparent ; moreover, in passing up the entire scale of verbal forms of delirium, from language that is completely incomprehensible to that which is to all appearances perfectly normal, observation reveals a marked continuity from patient to patient.

Often this incomprehensiveness is massive, so to speak; the recriminations of Emma or the constructions of Gabrielle will form a kind of verbal block, whose composition and structure are so unexpected that the ear alone can really be said to perceive them. It is impossible to take them down as dictation: for however automatic our stenography, we have always a vague understanding of what we write and an almost unconscious comprehension of it. If an absurdity slips into the dictated text, our attention is generally aroused, and the writing mechanism suddenly ceases to work. Indeed, that mechanism can hardly get started, and, consequently, our only recollection of these voluble declarations is a prodigious explosion of words and feelings, the shapeless débris of which we find scattered in our memory and, on reflection, see in them, *faute de mieux*, deliriant conceptions. But actually at this stage the delirium has, so to speak, passed beyond conceptual forms.

At other times the incomprehensibility is less striking, and in a sense we are better able to grasp it. In the middle of complaints which are undoubtedly deliriant but are expressed in terms which seem to be within the range of our experience, and therefore provide material for our imagination, Charles declares that he has felt a black ball pass through his head ; and quite suddenly we find ourselves beyond the comprehension or realization of this extraordinary sensation, at once cenesthetic and visual. In this form the incomprehensibility of pathological language is more instructive than in the previous case. It might have been attributed before, for want of a better explanation, to a momentary exaltation of feeling. But here it is in a process of development which we believe we are able to follow in detail, and in which the patient himself seems able to define his state in terms that allow us to represent it to ourselves approximately as a case of obvious incomprehensibility with no apparent modification in the accompanying affective tone.

Or again, as in the striking example of Bertha, pathological language presents more subtle difficulties. At first sight nothing seems more banal or less esoteric than the majority of expressions in which the mental disturbances are objectified when isolated from their context. Yet from the relationships and continuity that the conversation of the patient automatically establishes between these expressions, we begin to feel that it is only possible to arrive at a partial understanding of them through some sort of initiation into the original psychic conditions which determine their use. On examination, the terms which Bertha borrows from us are found not to stand for any system of representations analogous to ours, but to correspond to conceptual complexities of which we have no experience. Despite appearances she is really speaking what is to us a foreign language. In order to be understood, her most ordinary remarks need a very subtle translation, since they cannot be interpreted aright unless we bring back to a state of initial undifferentiation certain elements, the distinction between which has been so stressed by language that it appears to our thought as one of its fundamental conditions.

At the other extremity of the scale, too, we find Adrienne, Emma, Gabrielle, Charles and Bertha to have been undoubtedly delirious, and their language generally the expression of deliriant ideas. Here the situation is more difficult to judge. The hypochondriacal preoccupations of Adrienne, more by their localization than by their violence, come strangely near to certain organic or functional troubles which were diagnosed in objective examination, and give rise to intense and paradoxical motor and affective-motor reactions; we seem obliged to attribute them to the influence of a morbid conviction.

But is the fact that the patient complains of her health, though the complaints have nothing abnormal about them except their persistence and the absence of lesions or corresponding disturbances, sufficient to justify the charge of delirium? Admitting that we have here a case of deliriant conviction, we must yet notice that the language by which it expresses itself is never once clearly illogical, as in the other examples discussed, nor, at any rate at first sight, does it imply in internal or external experience those transpositions of representative value or the system of supernatural subordinations which generally indicate delirium. In the details of her complaints, Adrienne does not differ greatly from patients whom one would never dream of calling insane. The intensity of her affecto-motor and motor reactions, however, have led us to suspect that she falls into a category equivalent to that of delirium. So by showing that pathological language, even though it may appear to us as perfectly lucid, may yet in reality be quite unintelligible, we find our previous suspicion confirmed and justified.

It would seem as if we had here reached a point where the relationship of normal and morbid concepts is still sufficiently close to prevent their divergence from being betrayed in language ; but where pathological thought cannot safely reunite with experiences and representations that are perhaps no longer capable of being imposed on it. Beneath the profusion of images and metaphors which envelope the preoccupations of Adrienne with a luminous mist, does there not lie some fundamental disturbance of psychic activity? The analysis of this, in the light of what we learnt from other observations, might help us to understand the nature and character of morbid intellectual reactions before they develop into conceptions which are unquestionably deliriant.

This wealth of images and metaphors is not the exclusive privilege of Adrienne. It is almost the rule among patients. But sometimes, as with Adrienne, images and metaphors never cease to be considered as such, they are never given as an adequate expression of reality, they remain free of all marked association or transformation of delirium; sometimes, while appearing in a symbiotic relation with deliriant conceptions, they may yet, so to speak, remain parallel with them, and keep to a certain extent their figurative value; or, finally, they may be incorporated in the delirium until (fancy becoming fact) they lose their specific quality.

Metaphorical language is so much a normal form of discursive thought that it is born with it, and the greater part of the terms we employ are old images no longer in use. We never hesitate to employ them when exact words fail us for expressing what we feel and when direct expression seems incompletely satisfying to the particular exigencies of our thought. This resort to metaphor occurs naturally, almost unconsciously, and the image springs more or less immediately from the contact of our previous experience with new realities.

Thus, when we hear patients using and abusing metaphors it is quite natural to suppose that their mental situation is identical with ours on a similar occasion so that, if they employ a similar type of expression, it is because objective data are present to their consciousness which would excite in us analogous reactions.

A fair number of doctors and psychologists have thus been led to believe that disturbances of general sensibility play the dominant rôle in these cases. The complaints of the patients on the subject of their physical health are so original that one supposes they are bound to have felt in actual fact what it would seem we would have needed to feel in order to make the same complaints. But objective examination of visceral sensibility, extremely difficult in practice, has given results either negative or subject to many interpretations : and vaso-motor disturbances, such as cyanosis of the extremities, slowness of the pulse, or diminution of glandular excretions, which seem as though they should appear in consciousness as a modification of cenesthetic sensations, are met with in many other cases without producing the same effects. If, then, they are causes, they are not the sole causes ; and since at other times they may be absent altogether, they are not indispensable. Notwithstanding what has been claimed, the cenesthetic theory is a psychological hypothesis, and it is from this point of view that we must judge it.

Undoubtedly some of our patients make certain complaints almost identical with those we ourselves make; it seems difficult, therefore, not to admit behind them pains at least analogous to ours. Migraine, headaches, deafness, giddiness, the sensation of stifling or suffocation, oppression, embarrassment, dullness, palpitation, gastric distention after food; intercostal neuralgia, cramp, tinglings, prickings, twitchings of muscles, chills, rheumatism; pains in the forehead, the gums, the back of the neck, the throat, arms, chest, loins, stomach, knees, feet and ankles; internal trembling and general debility; such is a list of symptoms in Adrienne, Bertha, Charles, Dorothea and Emma.

It is certainly unusual to experience so many pains at once, and their very multiplicity is surprising; but this is no reason for ignoring the fact that when we suffer we talk of our sufferings in the same way. Nor do we wish to suggest that the metaphors of our patients are in general unfamiliar to us. For example, pains like an iron bar; the sensation of pressure, of a knife, or a hook, or of a cord being tightened (Adrienne); a feeling of heaviness (Bertha) ; of a weight in, or on, the head ; a feeling of emptiness, pains like lightning, and paralysis (Charles) ; the sensation of a heavy helmet on the head, sharp points, pin-pricks, and chilliness (Emma) ; a feeling of slackness and complete inertia (Fernande) ; these are certainly far-fetched metaphors, but they are nevertheless often used by normal people to describe functional and organic disorders. Here again, it is not their nature that surprises us but their profusion.

Frequently these metaphors, like Janus, have a double face. One we may call coenesthetic, and with that we are now familiar ; the other deliriant. Bertha speaks of her absence of elasticity and of the deadness of her skin, but at the same time she says she is a splendid anatomical subject, a real mummy. Emma declares that her limbs are dislocated, that her eyes will not open, that her head and body are empty, that she has been disembowelled, that she has difficulty in walking, that she cannot turn her head and eyes as before, and that she feels as if she were weighted down by someone. But this imagery only receives full value when seen in the light of her possession mania. Fernande thinks her eyelids close over holes, that she has no body, and even that she is dead: none the less, she too is a mummy, and an automatic machine. Images, comparisons, metaphors are lost in delirium like waves in the sea.

We are now at the very heart of the problem: must we admit that cenesthetic disorders have brought about delirium as a consequence of their effects, and have engendered complaints so natural that they unquestionably prove the objectivity of their cause? Or, on the other hand, should the continuity which the play of metaphors establishes between the complaints and the delirious conception lead us to suspect that the subjectivity of the delirium penetrates even to the heart of the complaints themselves, and forbids us to connect the cenesthetic modifications with them *a priori*, as would normally be the case? We will try to defend and give grounds for the second of these two opinions.

In the first place, when a clinical examination allows us to establish the existence of functional disorder or organic lesions, we find, strange though it may seem, that these disorders and lesions do not play the chief part in the preoccupations or delirium of the patients. The fact is trivial, but it is well worth recording. Bertha, for instance, did not bother about her colitis or the state of her genital organs, though these were painful during the examination. Nor did Charles trouble specially about the atrophy of his left optic disc. Adrienne paid very little attention to the probable inflammation of her fallopian tubes, and the numerous pains that she complained of, which might possibly have arisen from it, were so strangely situated and so unnatural that they were almost unrecognizable. If cenesthetic disorders play the rôle attributed to them, how can we explain why the patients whose whole pathological history shows, in conformity with theory, a predisposition to simple or deliriant cenesthetic affections, do not make use of the organic lesions and functional disorders as the chief structure for their preoccupations or delirium, though we may naturally suppose that these disorders involve a modification of cenesthesia?

Again, the cenesthetic theory supposes that the patients talk our language. As a matter of fact, this is open to discussion, for we are often uncertain as to the exact meaning of their complaints. For example, Charles thinks that there is something missing from his legs and from the tips of his fingers; we should normally suppose this to be a cenesthetic disorder, since in our case we should be aware of the trouble through our sensibility; and when he cannot unbend his fingers as before, we assume, since a motor factor is here involved, some disturbance of his kinesthesia. But are we justified in assuming such a cenesthetic disturbance either central or peripheral? When objects appear changed to Charles, it is, according to him, because he is not able to make use of them as before; it is his lack of will-power and courage and his inability to work that are at fault. Might it not be this lack of will-power that is shown in the inability to extend his fingers, and in the feeling that there is something missing from their tips—a disorder with a subjective and objective expression at one and the same time? This is only a conjecture, but a very plausible conjecture, after what our observations have taught us of the imperceptible transitions produced in the consciousness of patients between the groups of concepts that normal thought uses for dealing with reality.

Again, Charles talks of obstruction and displacement of his brain, which feels as if it were not there. This would be a cenesthetic affair if we were quite sure that he was talking of his organic state and not his moral activity, but we have seen that we have no justification for being so positive. The uncertainty and the paradox of the situation culminate in the statement that he is "worn out", "exhausted", "finished", despite his excellent physical health, for he seems to dispute the integrity of his cenesthetic sensations by metaphors which necessitate the existence of cenesthetic disorders. Material images are most familiar to us ; in general, the organic is expressed by comparison with the inorganic, and thoughts by comparison with life ; we imagine that by materializing our sensations, sentiments, and ideas, we understand them better. But it is dangerous to take these comparisons literally.

Finally, even in cases where it seems that we can actually construct the syllogism which led the patient from cenesthetic disorders to deliriant conceptions, more often that not we find that we are deceived by some appearance and that in fact reality cannot be interpreted in this fashion. Gabrielle, in her delirium of pregnancy, spoke of abdominal pains, which provided her with evidence for her assertions. It would be natural to assume that her delirium arose from the internal sensations that she experienced. This was not so, however, for by her own avowal these sensations had nothing in common with the pains of ordinary pregnancy ; they only had that particular character because the deliriant conceptions decreed it. Cenesthetic disorders, then, are not the cause of delirium, since they derive all their significance from it. It even seems likely that this significance is wholly responsible for their existence, and that in the absence of such interpretations the patients would pay but little attention to them. In any case we can be sure that cenesthetic disorders are not of first importance in these cases.

Now if we consider these deliriant conceptions abstractedly and listen to Gabrielle talking of her abdominal pains and to her complaints of shivering, trembling and 'shooting' sensations and of a kind of rivet that she feels in her loins, comparing her sufferings to the effects of thunder and the weight of lead, we feel as though we might be listening to Adrienne, to whom we now return after this long détour. There is the same metaphorical richness that was incompletely explained by hypothetical cenesthetic disorders in the former case, without the introduction of deliriant preoccupations. Are they sufficient in the second case, where in place of delirium we have diffuse hypochondriacal obsessions which do not greatly overstep the bounds of thought and logic?

To accept this hypothesis we would have to make something mysterious out of cenesthetic disorders, something which baffles our experience and necessitates a desperate effort of analysis to explain it. But surely it is nothing of the kind. We have all experienced cenesthetic disturbances: our headaches and our neuralgia, our vague and erratic pains, are all so many shocks to our cenesthesis. And how do we behave in regard to them? We say that we are suffering, and in such and such a place. Usually this is enough to satisfy us. If the pain is unusual and unexpected we say we do not know what is the matter with us, and speak of an indefinable pain. If it has particular characteristics we go so far as to compare it with the feeling of a bar pressing on us, or of a vice or gimlet. If the pain continues we submit to it more or less with resignation. We are more disturbed by its consequences and its actual presence than by its nature. The fact that it exists seems to define it sufficiently; we are interested in other things than in defining it, and do not exhaust ourselves in providing images and metaphors for this purpose.

But with our patients it is quite different. They never seem satisfied with the way in which they have described their state, and they will multiply their expressions *ad infinitum*. Of course they have their favourite formulae, but they renew them and enrich them at each fresh consultation, so much so that one is never sure of having all the varieties. It is as if all around their cenesthetic impressions there were a profusion of thoughts continually dwelt on, and metaphors endlessly amplified, similar to those surrounding representations that have become obsessions. In the normal individual an idea, however unexpected it may be, never becomes an obsession; nor do our cenesthetic disorders, however strange and painful they may be, goad us to that frenzy of interpretation which we have found in all our patients, and with particular intensity in Adrienne. However much we may be the victims of deception, there will always be some category of past experience into which an idea or a new impression will fall.

Why are our patients not content with as brief a description as we are when dealing with these so-called cenesthetic disorders? That is what the cenesthetic theory does not succeed in explaining, except by invoking a 'predisposition' which begs the question, since in its absence cenesthetic disorders would be without effect. It is precisely this that we must first explain, since it is not in the cenesthetic disorders of which we all have experience, but in the way in which they react, that our patients differ from us. So we are surely justified in concluding that the cenesthetic theory, the issue of a psychological hypothesis, fails in the psychological explanation of facts which it professes to elucidate.

Perhaps we shall better realize the fecundity of images and metaphors which become ever more apparent to us as an essential characteristic of our patient if, in the realm of psychology, we content ourselves with simply being psychologists. For instance, the more objective our knowledge, the fewer the images and metaphors in its expression : we find no rhetorical phrases in geometry. On the other hand, images and metaphors are frequently found in literature and poetry, and, above all, where the theme, being essentially subjective, resists discursive treatment and evades the empty generality of direct formulation. In short, images and metaphors make an appeal to the intuition, in default of the intellect, when this is weighted down, so to speak, by its conceptual armature and allows itself to be outdone by the flying multiplicity of the real.

Images and metaphors also show us that our demand for analysis is confronted by difficulties that conceptual distribution cannot deal with, so that it tries to obtain satisfaction by a series of comparisons more and more adequate, whose accumulation ultimately gives us a feeling, rather than knowledge by intellectual processes, of the irreducible reality round which they jostle.

This profusion of images and metaphors, and this insurmountable need for analysis, are met with in our patients as in the artist and the poet. Is it not possible that the cenesthetic states, to which we pay so little attention, may seem to them as difficult a problem and one as worthy of a solution as are the most subtle movements of individual sensibility in the eyes of the élite ? But this is only a hypothesis which requires confirmation. It is sufficient to have realized for the moment that intellectual reactions, in their most attenuated form, are to be explained not in terms of any particular character of certain psychical states, but rather by the attitude that consciousness takes with regard to these states.

The study of these first intellectual reactions was a natural pathway to the study of delirium, since the objectivization of images and the actualization of metaphors (as observation of Charles, Bertha, Emma and Fernande testifies) lead us straight to the heart of deliriant conceptions. There is, as Kant said, a sort of transition from judgments of

perception to judgments of experience, from the subjective to the objective. And it is impossible to over-emphasize the importance of this transitional stage, for its outcome is the begetting of a new experience, paradoxical at first sight, since it is founded on judgments of perception. But though this transition is of frequent occurrence, the case of Adrienne is sufficient to show that it is not a clinical necessity.